Isn't It A Wonder!

Isn't It A Wonder!

Carrie Lou Goddard

Illustrated by Leigh Grant

Abingdon Press

Nashville and New York

Isn't It a Wonder!

Copyright © 1976 by Abingdon Press

All Rights Reserved

Printed in the United States of America

Library of Congress Cataloging in Publication Data

GODDARD, CARRIE LOU.   ISN'T IT A WONDER

   SUMMARY: Examines the many wonders that God has
created—the sun, trees, grass, snow, people, and much more.
   1. Creation—Juvenile literature. [1. Creation]
I. Grant, Leigh. II. Title.

BS651.G68   231.1   75-15664

ISBN 0-687-19715-5

Dedicated to three very
special little girls—
Rebekah,
Deborah, and
Tabitha

Isn't it a wonder how God created

the sun to shine on
the grass, on the
trees, on the
houses, and on
me when it is day—

the moon to shine on
the grass, on the trees,
on the houses, and
on me when it
is night?

Isn't it a wonder how God creates

the snow that
falls when the
days are cold—

the wind that blows
the trees and me,
the rain that falls
with a splash?

Isn't it a wonder how God creates

flowers that bloom—

trees that give shade—

grass to walk on—

trees with fruit to eat?

Isn't it a wonder how God creates

birds that swim in the water?

birds that fly in the air—

Isn't it a wonder how God creates

frisky animals like dogs
to run with—

cuddly animals like kittens
to play with—

large animals like cows to
give milk to drink—

strong animals like ponies
to ride?

Isn't it a wonder how God creates people

with eyes to use for seeing—

with a nose to use for smelling—

with a tongue to use for tasting—

with ears to use for hearing—

with a body that can feel?

Isn't it a wonder how God created me

with arms to reach
and hands to hold—

with feet and legs
to walk, to run,
to climb—

with a body that has
a back and a stomach—

with a head that
has eyes for seeing,
ears for hearing, a
tongue for tasting and
talking, and a
nose for smelling?

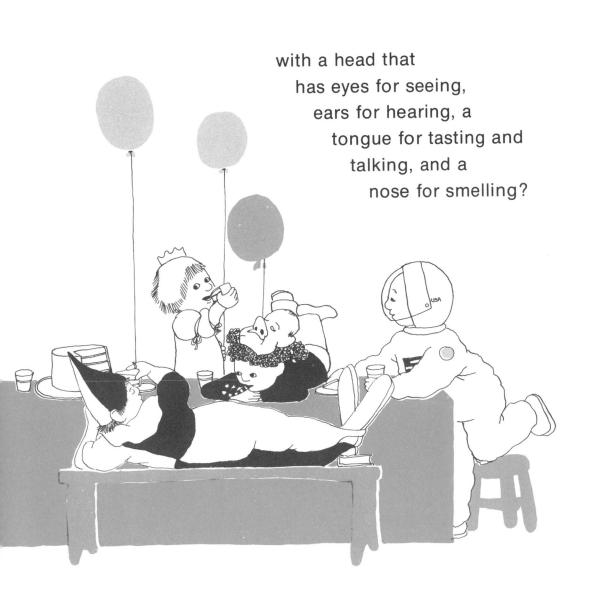

Isn't it a wonder how God creates

parents who love children,

grandparents or friends who
love children—

brothers and sisters
and friends with
whom to play?

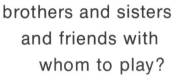

Yes, everything God creates is a wonder!

"And God saw that it was good."
Genesis 1:10